The Embrace:

Diego Rivera and Frida Kahlo

Poems by

Carolyn Kreiter-Foronda

For Lee, with admiration of your talent as a poet and teacher. Thank you for your support.

With cheer & love,
Carolyn Kreiter-Foronda

San Francisco Bay Press 2013

The Embrace: Diego Rivera and Frida Kahlo

Printed in the United States of America

EDITOR: Robert P. Arthur
COVER AND BOOK DESIGN: Jeff Hewitt

COVER PHOTOGRAPH: Frida Kahlo, *The Love Embrace of the Universe, the Earth (Mexico), Diego, Me and Señor Xólotl, El abrazo de amor del universo, la tierra (México), Diego, yo y el señor Xólotl,* 1949
Oil on Masonite, 70 x 60.5 cm
The Jacques and Natasha Gelman Collection of the 20th Century Mexican Art and The Vergel Foundation
Mexico City, D.F., Mexico
©2012 Banco de México Diego Rivera Frida Kahlo Museums Trust, Mexico, D.F. / Artists Rights Society (ARS), New York
Photo Credit: Erich Lessing / Art Resource, NY

MURAL, PART I: Diego Rivera, *The Embrace (El abrazo)*, 1923
Court of Labor, Level 1, East Wall, 4.78 x 1.83 m.
Secretaría de Educación Pública
Mexico City, D.F., Mexico
©2012 Banco de México Diego Rivera Frida Kahlo Museums Trust, Mexico, D.F. / Artists Rights Society (ARS), New York
Photo Credit: Schalkwijk / Art Resource, NY

PAINTING, PART II: Frida Kahlo, *The Two Fridas (Las dos Fridas)*, 1939
Oil on canvas, 5′ 8½″ x 5′ 8½″
Museo Nacional de Arte Moderno, Instituto Nacional de Bellas Artes
Mexico City, D.F., Mexico
©2012 Banco de México Diego Rivera Frida Kahlo Museums Trust, Mexico, D.F. / Artists Rights Society (ARS), New York
Photo Credit: Schalkwijk / Art Resource, NY

AUTHOR PHOTOGRAPH, BOOK COVER:
Marie Harris

SFBP First paperback edition

ISBN 978-0-98-282956-1

San Francisco Bay Press
522 Spotswood Ave C5
Norfolk Va 23517

Acknowledgments

These poems or earlier versions of them—some with different titles—first appeared in the following publications:

Apropos Literary Journal: Featured segment—"Frida and Black Cat," "The Two Fridas (I): On the Border Line between Mexico and the United States," and "Hymn: The Embrace"

Autumn Sky Poetry: "Frida Dialogues with Her Heart" and "The Skeleton on Top of Frida's Four-Poster Bed"

Connotation Press: An Online Artifact: "The Crematorium at the Panteón Civil de Dolores," "Frida Kahlo," "Offerings, Day of the Dead," and "Bread"

Delaware Poetry Review: Excerpts from *Murals*— "Night of the Poor" and "City Festival, Day of the Dead"

Fjords Arts and Literary Review: Featured segment—"Zapatista Landscape: The Guerilla," "La Casa Azul," "The Two Fridas (VI): Broken Column and Plaster Cast," and "Frida and Mask"

Lady Jane's Miscellany: "The Milliner and His Hats"

Nimrod International Journal: "Halley's Comet," and "Diego and Calla Lilies"

Poet Lore: "The Two Fridas (III): Sitting on a Wicker Bed with Ceramic Doll"

r.kv.r.y. quarterly literary journal: "Young Dimas Rosas, Deceased at Age Three" and "Frida and Wet Nurse"

Terrain.org: A Journal of the Built & Natural Environments: "Portrait of Luther Burbank" and "On the Pedregal: Frida and Vines"

The Comstock Review: "The Two Fridas (IV)"

The Poet's Domain: "Letter to Diego"

Tipton Poetry Journal: "Entering the Mine" and "The Two Fridas (V): The Wounded Table"

"Diego and Calla Lilies," "Leaving the Mine," "Night of the Rich," "Stone Worker and Creviced Rock," "The Two Fridas (II): Collage, Manhattan," "The Two Fridas (VII): Paint Me Flying," and "Deer Running" appear in *An Endless Skyway: Poetry from the State Poets Laureate*, edited by Caryn Mirriam-Goldberg, Marilyn L. Taylor, Denise Low, and Walter Bargen, Ice Cube Books, 2011.

A Spanish translation of "Letter to Diego" appears under the title, "Carta a Diego" in the anthology, *Cauteloso engaño del sentido,* edited by Rei Berroa, as part of Colección Libros de la Luna, Vol. No. 2, Santo Domingo, República Dominicana, 2007.

"The Two Fridas (IV)" was selected as a Poem of Special Merit by the Editorial Board of *The Comstock Review*, Vol. 23, No. 2, Fall/Winter Awards issue, 2009.

"The Crematorium at the Panteón Civil de Dolores" was a finalist in *Cutthroat, A Journal of the Arts* 2010 Joy Harjo Poetry Contest.

"Frida and Wet Nurse," originally published under the title "My Nurse and I," was nominated by *r.kv.r.y. quarterly literary journal* for a Pushcart Prize.

"The Two Fridas (VI): Broken Column and Plaster Cast" was nominated by *Fjords Arts and Literary Review* for a Pushcart Prize.

"Portrait of Luther Burbank" and "On the Pedregal: Frida and Vines" are accompanied by audio clips at *www.terrain.org.*, where the poems were published under the titles, "Two Voices: Wizard of Horticulture" and "Two Voices: Roots."

Connotation Press: An Online Artifact featured an interview with poetry editor Kaite Hillenbrand and the author in Issue II, Volume III, October 2011.

r.kv.r.y. quarterly literary journal featured an interview with editor Mary Akers and the author in Vol. VI, No. 3, Fall 2011.

I extend my appreciation to Harry N. Abrams, Inc., to Dover Publications, Inc., and to Chronicle Books for granting permission to use quotations from these sources:

THE DIARY OF FRIDA KAHLO English translation copyright ©1995 by Harry N. Abrams, Inc. [Used by permission of Harry N. Abrams, Inc., New York. All rights reserved.]

Rivera, Diego. *My Art, My Life: An Autobiography (with Gladys March).* Mineola, New York: Dover Publications, Inc., 1991, pp. 41 and 83. ISBN: 0-486-26938-8

Zamora, Martha. *Frida Kahlo: The Brush of Anguish.* Trans. Marilyn Sode. San Francisco: Chronicle Books LLC, ©1990, p. 126. [Used with permission of Chronicle Books LLC, San Francisco. Visit ChronicleBooks.com]

I am most grateful to the Banco de México and its agent ARS (Artists Rights Society) for granting the rights to reproduce the artwork of Frida Kahlo and Diego Rivera. I also express appreciation to Art Resource for providing print rights for the art images. I offer a heartfelt thanks to the two agents who guided me through the process: Maria Fernanda Meza (ARS) and Robbi Siegel (Art Resource).

Frida Kahlo, *The Love Embrace of the Universe, the Earth (Mexico), Diego, Me and Señor Xolótl* (cover image)
©2012 Banco de México Diego Rivera Frida Kahlo Museums Trust, Mexico, D.F. / Artists Rights Society (ARS), New York
Photo Credit: Erich Lessing / Art Resource, NY

Diego Rivera, *The Embrace* (Section I)
©2012 Banco de México Diego Rivera Frida Kahlo Museums Trust, Mexico, D.F. / Artists Rights Society (ARS), New York
Photo Credit: Schalkwijk / Art Resource, NY

Frida Kahlo, *The Two Fridas* (Section II)
©2012 Banco de México Diego Rivera Frida Kahlo Museums Trust, Mexico, D.F. / Artists Rights Society (ARS), New York
Photo Credit: Schalkwijk / Art Resource, NY

I express my deepest appreciation to my husband, Patricio Gómez-Foronda, who accompanied me on trips to Mexico City, served as translator on guided tours of museums, and offered invaluable insight into Hispanic/Latino customs, traditions, and beliefs. I extend gratitude to Raúl Puga for an extensive tour of the Secretaría de Educación Pública in Mexico City, where I first viewed the murals of Diego Rivera. I am indebted to my editor, Robert P. Arthur, for his insightful critique of the poems and his continued support of my work; Jeff Hewitt for his advice and expertise in designing the book's layout and cover; and my friend and sister poet, Marie Harris, for the author photo printed on the back cover. For their generous endorsements, I thank Shonda Buchanan and Joyce Brinkman. Finally, I owe gratitude to members of my poetry group for their unwavering support of this book: Dianne Jordan, Nancy Powell, and Ann Shalaski.

Contents

II FRIDA KAHLO

For Patricio Gómez-Foronda

and in loving memory of
Victor William Kreiter, Jr.
1942-2011

Preface

The first time I saw the paintings of world-renowned artists Diego Rivera and Frida Kahlo at El Museo del Barrio in New York City, I knew a book of poems was in the making. Prominent works, such as Kahlo's autobiographical *Self-Portrait with Bed* and Rivera's classic *Calla Lily Vendor*—both from The Jacques and Natasha Gelman Collection—led to journal jottings, which soon transformed themselves into monologues in the voices of the painters themselves. For the next few years, I researched the lives of these influential Mexican artists, whose voices I heard each time I stared into their portraits.

Part I of *The Embrace* centers on Diego Rivera's expansive artistic vision. Throughout his life, this prolific painter was well-known for promoting revolutionary ideals, which still bear large-scale relevance today. I gained insight into Rivera's intent by studying his paintings and immense murals at various museums in Mexico City and its suburbs. The murals that captivated me the most appear in the Secretaría de Educación Pública (Ministry of Public Education). Here, Rivera's art depicts the indigenous people at work, their merrymaking at festivals while also exposing vices, such as the abuse of power by the upper class. These enduring murals inspired a ten-poem sequence in the voices of figures immortalized on the walls of this monumental building. The book's first section concludes with a series of monologues in the voices of Rivera's four wives—Angelina Beloff (common-law wife), Lupe Marín, Frida Kahlo, and Emma Hurtado. Collectively, the monologues offer a glimpse into Rivera's personal life, his inability to remain faithful, and his unwavering loyalty to his art.

Part II evolved after exploring La Casa Azul, or the Blue House, where Frida Kahlo was born and lived most of her life, eventually succumbing to disabilities caused by a horrific bus crash when she was eighteen. The accident left the iconic and enigmatic artist physically and emotionally crippled when a handrail pierced her body. As I wandered from room to room of the Blue House, Kahlo spoke to me through riveting self-portraits, diary entries, letters, photographs, native pottery, a wheelchair, medicines, and art supplies. The home's ambiance and vivid indigo walls evoked images of lively parties and flamboyant affairs. On entering her bedroom, I sensed the pain of her childhood bout with polio. I felt the turmoil of her two marriages to Rivera—first in 1929 and again in 1940.

Both sections of *The Embrace* contain art-inspired poems that explore the dualities I envisioned in the relationship of this eminent couple and noted in their artwork. Kahlo, herself, developed dual identities, most likely to cope with the difficulties of Rivera's infidelities, of her disability, and her inability to bear children. To capture these dualities, I created simultaneous or two-voice poems—some spoken by Rivera, Kahlo, or an informed narrator. Other speakers include a doll, a mask, calla lilies, vines, or another symbolic object assuming an imagined life of its own in a vibrant painting. In each of these poems, the voices—one in standard text, the other italicized—can be read separately down the page. A third poem emerges when the two voices are read together—i.e., horizontally across the page—with the intent of broadening and enriching the interpretation of a painting.

As the book developed, "the embrace" enlarged to include Frida's beloved dogs, monkeys, jewels, and Diego's mistresses. For both artists, the act of painting was the ultimate embrace —one that continues to enthrall gallery-goers allured by the beauty of calla lilies or by the intriguing glare of a woman too seductive to ignore. I invite the readers of this book to discover the embrace of the universe, which held Rivera and Kahlo together for an extended period of artistic discovery and intrigue.

Carolyn Kreiter-Foronda

Diego Rivera, *The Embrace (El abrazo)*, 1923
Mural, Court of Labor, Level 1, East Wall, 4.78 x 1.83 m.
Secretaría de Educación Pública, Mexico City, D.F., Mexico

Photo Credit: Schalkwijk / Art Resource, NY

I

DIEGO RIVERA

1886—1957

"I... discovered an enormous artistic reservoir. It was of the kind that enabled the American genius Walt Whitman to create, on a grander scale than anyone had before, the poetry of the common people, working, suffering, fighting, seeking joy, living and dying." [1]

Diego Rivera
My Art, My Life: An Autobiography
(with Gladys March)

Diego and Calla Lilies

Kneeling on a petate mat,
The basket, deep enough,
an Indian woman sits upright,
supports our long, firm stems.
her unclothed frame scented.
We settle into clots of dirt.
Is it sandalwood? Mahogany?
Like absinthe, we intoxicate
I paint her broad shoulders:
the artist who shapes the woman's arms
earthy dabs of nutmeg, hyacinth
with the mastery of sun
so she can thrive like the flowers,
so she can embrace us.
so she can feel the florets swell.
Her hands, smelling of freesia,
Soon, she will rise out of shadows
reach out to our trumpets blaring
to gather bluets, yarrows.
as though she hears a mariachi horn,
What is happiness, if not this need?
feels our desire to return to marshes,
See how she rests—a saint—holding
watery fields, shallow pools far from
pearls, luminous as fire?
the lover who approaches a street vendor—
Now, maybe you understand who I am.
scissor snips ringing through the market,
In the city, in the valleys,
fleshy tubes and arrow-shaped leaves
I wander in search of legends
rolled into wrapping paper, sold for a few pesos,
to begin anew. Oh, these calla lilies!
the blooms' swanlike hearts pounding.

Stone Worker and Creviced Rock

Thick-built, solid, I am all man,
Virile,

my woman says, rough-hewn
a pillar

and durable as the bits
of gray,

I hammer from this
creviced

block. The ground
like magma,

swells with unwanted chunks,
I hold still,

shattered by blows, every stroke
counting

releasing a thud as I pound
the chips

and lose myself in a dance,
broken loose

my arm hurling downward,
from my side

pulling back into air
and tossed

with the force

to the ground—

of each crushing thwack.

flawed,

Late at night, I hear the echo

he thinks,

of a mallet's smack.

striking again,

The walls I build

splintering

can't compare to the statues

pieces

I shape in my mind: divine deities

of my soul

from basalt, waiting.

until there's

One day I will carry

little more than

volcanic rocks home,

fragments to

carve and burnish,

break, yet

set free what is trapped

my spirit soars

inside the crude blocks.
as he smooths, polishes,

In the quarries
places me

I can hear
on the wall's crest.

voices singing.

The Milliner and His Hats

Laid out like sweets, these saucy hats
the ladies wear like rouge on cheeks

Why do you pinch us?
Before a mirror you smirk

and dream of houses, dressed
with furniture, curvy as rims

as if our souls can't see your lust.
Look, mister, women want lilac,

topped with ribbons,
feathers, pins.

chenille or roses, cherry
clusters: Jazz. Jive.

The little flirts, begging
for money, lure men to buy

Toss aside these ribbons,
floppy as lily bells.

my star creations available
in navy, jade, webs of hot pink.

Can't you hear our sighs?
We yearn for cabarets:

How like them to entice their lovers
with camellias opening leggy blooms,

> *dancers clicking their heels, vintage*
> *plumes wooing the feisty air.*

stiff tongues licking the brims,
the veiling, and fashionable trim.

> *Come. Tease the notes out*
> *of our patterned throats.*

Here's a fine fit with racy furls.
Silly girls, please your men with this.

> *Tame this slippery fabric.*
> *Pleat these divine threads.*

Halley's Comet

In the Gallery of the San Carlos, Diego Rivera's first one-man exhibition opened on November 20, 1910—the same day the Mexican Revolution broke out with an uprising against the dictator, Porfirio Díaz.

I

You gloat at the Opening. Regal, prim,
the dictator's wife buys six paintings
and toasts your success. *The Valley
of Ambles* and *The Tranquil Hours*
belie the tension mounting outside
the city among *campesinos*. To think
that years later you would lie, claiming
you intended to assassinate Díaz,
claiming Lenin needed you abroad
to arbitrate among Mexican factions.
Could you not own up to the truth?
In May, I soared through skies over
Mexico, warned your countrymen
to heed the unrest. Some called my
fiery appearance an omen. You,
Diego, were in Paris. With an eye
averted, you painted long into night.

II

Look at you, *muy importante*
in a tailored suit. Your bulging
eyes pierce holes into a critic
who barely notices your art.
Go ahead. Cast him off
as you later would Angelina,
who bore your son, and Marevna,

mother of the baby you labeled
child of the armistice. Do not
ignore me. Others before you
have been this careless. In 66 AD,
I steered ships off course.
1066, I flew over England,
cursed Harold of Hastings.
In the 1300s, I posed as Giotto's
Star of Bethlehem, curved
like a saber over the Nativity.
Each time I reappear, I make
a more powerful showing.

III

Egotistical. Quarrelsome.
The devil is in the room, Diego.
Mask after mask you wear
like armor. As a boy you opened
the stomach of a pregnant mouse,
played with your brother's corpse—
you claimed—at a wake.
What do you say now to a child
soldier who bears arms, stumbles
over bodies in barren fields?
How many etchings, drawings,
oils did you bring here to please
la crema de la sociedad?
In a corner of the gallery, patrons
surround one of your masterpieces,
admire the rotund face staring back.
You lift a glass to the hostess, guests,
to the long life of Don Porfirio.
How can you ignore the cries
of the dead rattling the windows
of this sumptuous hall?

Zapatista Landscape: The Guerilla

With a swagger, he enters,
a revolutionary toting a gun,
cartridge belt swiveling, swung low

about the hips. Near the center
of the canvas, I dab white dots,
add a pointillist eye over a half-circle

of black so he can search for haciendas
and spy snipers hidden in dense
foliage. How well he knows this valley:

viridian trees, mountains lifting
into a radiating sky, volcanoes:
the anointed guardians of Mexico.

Pausing, he wraps a serape tighter,
positions his rifle upright for quick
defense, the lush vista a reminder

of lost territory, his indigenous
half-brothers forced into slavery.
I paint the gun's shadow white,

scumble green over a patch of enemy
ground, layer details.
His sombrero floats above the trees,

elevates his vision so he can guard against
the theft of village property.
He bows, gives thanks for his heritage:

a *mestizo* free of bondage. I apply cobalt,
maroon, dun-gray, olive
to enhance the mystique of the land

so he will fight for the right to stand
here and breathe the sierra's purity
filling with its own radiance.

Murals

In 1923 Rivera began painting 124 frescoes on three floors of the Ministry of Education building in Mexico City. These murals reflect the Mexican people at work, their land, struggles, triumphs, and festivals. Rivera longed for a day when everyone would exist in harmony, without class distinctions.

I Entering the Mine

A rooster's crow swallows what's left of night.
The lantern I clutch flickers as I enter
the hill's gashed belly.

I offer a blessing to the underworld, pray
to its ruler. *No need to take chances*,
I tell myself, swinging a pick

into rich veins of silver. The stench
of Devil's breath fills my lungs.
I cough. I remember Papá

hovering over my bed and kissing
my forehead. "Don't follow me
into the mines," he warned.

"The fumes will turn your lungs to stone."
A five-year-old, I squeezed
his hand like a treasure.

At fourteen, I toiled in fields, built up
my muscles until they commanded
crops like rain filaments.

At eighteen, I followed Papá through narrow
streets to the mines, bowed my head
before descending,

each of my brothers heaving a wooden beam
as if carrying the cross of Jesús.
Now, I lean against a rugged wall,

take shallow breaths, tell myself the stale air
won't harm me. I stare into darkness,
see again my father slumped

in a corner like a pile of dirt. This time
he doesn't speak but floats
toward me, a banner unfurling.

From its seams, water pours over crude,
rough nuggets. I touch his blackened
fingers, shout his name

into the moonless night as we lift him rung
by rung up the ladder. His lantern flares
like fire. *Mi padre. Mi padre.*

II Leaving the Mine

Again you search me.
With your cartridge belt
clanging against your hip,

you are no better. You probe
each miner until someone
hands over the stolen silver,

which you'll steal yourself
when no one's looking.
I am nothing to you,

a poor worker longing
for a few pesos. Bread
the color of your shirt.

Beans lampblack. Corn
sweetened by the sun-drenched
rays I long for

in the tunnels of this open pit.
I raise my arms into granite
sky, my frame posed

like a crucifix, my sandaled feet bleeding.
Beneath your leather boots,
my brother clings to a rope-

and-timber ladder, his face ashen.
Hunched over, you frisk my flanks.
The stench of tobacco

carries me back. My father had arrived
home late. "A boulder the size
of this room," he said,

"collapsed into fistfuls of ore."
As someone dragged Papá
through a narrow hole, he closed

his eyes and dreamed of gold and silver
ready to mold into coins, each adorned
with the coat of arms:

an eagle gripping a snake in its beak.
Hoisted to the surface and stripped,
he barely felt the hands

of the light-skinned man run up and down
his naked thighs. Papá should
have shaped the metals

into shining swords, sharpened them
until they slid like a curse
through the guard's ribs.

III Hymn: The Embrace

Embrace the land, my brothers.
It will sing to you of stony hills
sheltering the tremulous night,

of rivers, belling slopes, a flute's
voice in moon's wail.
Sing of you, *mis hermanos,*

come together in the saintly dark.
Embrace the land gone fallow, scorched
fields, dust-laden rows.

They will sing to you of ill-starred
crops, the curdle of worms,
brambles, an owl's screech.

Sing of a farmer's howl
in the dead of day.
Embrace the land, gentle

peasant and urban worker.
It will sing of consoling rains,
the descent of amber rays.

Sing of a halo in the shape
of a sombrero wreathing
your heads, bowed as one.

IV The Festival Workers Address Corn

With the promise of plenty,
we haul you from churned
soil and carpet streets

with your silken hair and seeds.
We weave rustling leaves
around poles adorned

with daisies, yellow-eyed,
illuminated at dusk.
Wearing flaxen hats

and costumes, we twirl you
into an ornate cross
with an artisan's touch.

Your tassels stir amid melodies
of street musicians
singing a language

that ascends the high-pitched
strumming of guitars,
a language, clear-

voiced, that settles in fields
far from where we gather
with children

to praise your bounty,
shimmering like wings
in primal light.

V Offerings, Day of the Dead

There's nothing morbid about death,
yet here your family sits: spectral,
downcast as if the spirits

are late, figures adorned, ornamental
paper cut like Posada's skeletons,
like lace and strung

in bourgeois finery while tapers
burn, fill the cemetery
with the absence of praise,

lost promises on an altar. Weightless,
they enter through cracks
of earth, become their former

selves while you, content to share
this bounty, pray and offer
pescado y pollo picante

to deceased relatives who'd rather
once a year eat sugar skulls
with icing, with the scent

of incense adorning the bones.
Stop frowning. Caress them.
La calavera catrina taps

on headstones as the sportive angels
take down the imposing wreaths,
snuff out candles, admire

their portraits tidied with a wealth
of marigolds for as long as
danza de la muerte lasts.

VI City Festival, Day of the Dead

Strumming tunes, we swing high
above the crowd and click
our heels in a festive salsa.

A farmer and revolutionist strut
beside me. We call ourselves
The Dancing Calaveras.

From the stage, we see it all—crooked
bankers, heady poets, *campesinos*
in town for a good time.

Behind a food stand, an Indian woman
in frilly yellow serves revelers
pulque from a large red jar.

Another in pigtails grills tacos
while merrymakers, bleary-eyed, stare
into space as if their pricey

pearls, dresses, heels hadn't landed them
the high-rollers they'd hoped for.
Tonight carousers will entice

our souls to come alive—candies,
bottles of tequila placed on graves,
lit-up like altars.

Wearing skeletal masks, they
should learn from us.
No one pulls our strings.

This fancy music's not for them, but for us—
los muertos, who nourish on trinkets
and bread offerings

that bring us back once a year
to let the living know
we are worth something.

VII The Burning of the Judases

Hanging in effigy, a capitalist
dressed in black extends
his arms: repentant criminal,

glasses atop his stubby snout.
A born sinner, scheming,
he hands out cash to thin

the crowd. Astride an armored horse,
the general beside him fires a pistol
with one hand, wields a sword

with the other while a holy priest,
consumed in smoke, sways
like an ambushed bandit.

I pry loose a handful of paving stones
from the street, hurl them
at the giant totems: lying Judases

swinging back and forth. "Betrayal,"
the angry crowd shouts as the fiesta turns
into a brawl. Fire engulfs

the hollowed-out bodies. Suspended
from a rope, the charcoaled figures swim
in midair, then drop to earth.

I pick up the general's gun,
still smoldering. With the heel
of my boot, I flatten the papier-

mâché torso, kick it asunder.
"It's over," I yell above cheers
of the throng. Look at them,

withering corpses, heaped in a pile,
their lies and deceits
gone up in smoke.

VIII Night of the Rich

I offer her a sip of champagne,
which slides down her throat
like liquid gold. Her eyes

glaze over as if she's dreaming
of easy dollars and a *casa grande*
she can keep. In a slinky dress

alabaster as moon, she leans
toward me, hair pulled in a bun:
decadent crown of jewels.

The room stifling with cigar smoke,
I know what I'm doing is wrong,
but like spending a wad of cash,

I can't resist the urge to force
myself on a *señorita* in heels.
Outside, the shouts of revolutionists

mount. I close my eyes, become
a young bank teller longing
for more, the city racing by

like a frantic bird. It's come to this:
money buys a young *inocente.*
I lure her into my den, teach her

the power of *pesos duros*.
Like a sunflower unfolding, she circles
before me, her breath scented

with lavender. The magic's in the drink.
Her voice fluid as water, she lies down,
claims I'm her salvation, then shows

off dainty hands, covering my limbs
with magnolia blossoms until I release
a sharp cry. We all scheme

before death's arm slithers
around our shoulders and relaxes
our grip on luxurious dreams.

IX Night of the Poor

As a girl, I slept on the street
in a cardboard box. At four,
I learned how to beg.

If I spied a well-dressed *señora* leaving
the market, a loaf of bread
tucked under each arm,

I lowered my eyes and pleaded,
"*Pan fresco.* Fresh bread, *por favor*,"
my pudgy legs no match

for the elegant limbs of the tall lady.
I glanced toward the sun for luck,
the giant disk, burnt orange.

On a good day I'd wave coins
above my head, drop them into
my mother's palms like piñons.

"*María, Madre de Dios*," she'd bless me
and tell me to feel proud.
At night, surrounded by family,

I'd curl up in Mama's arms.
Stars covered me with bougainvillea,
and as I dreamed, the pink

petals would become adobe bricks,
walls, and windows of the house
my father had promised me

when I turned seven. Cherries trickled
          down from the heavens. I plucked one
                    and wished time would stand

still so I could watch my parents
          and brothers enter the new home,
                    which opened onto a corridor

of doors. "Don't wake," I told myself
          as voices from the real houses
                    grew louder.

On the sidewalk where I slept,
          the noise passed over
                    like a choir of angels.

X Bread

"Now they have bread for all,
the naked, the men at the bottom . . ."[2]
From: *"Corrido de la Revolución"*

Partake of the wheat.
Break into morsels and eat.
Break grain, whole meal,

graham, rye. Tongues of flour
baked to a nut-brown.
Bread splits in two

at the fire's pleasure. Bread of the fields,
scattered to crows and tossed
to the aqua birds.

With the first taste will come
pineapples, papayas, peaches
the size of your hand, milk

flowing from a split coconut's cup.
With the taste will come a platterful
of cheeses, jugs of honey

the shade of umber flesh. Give praise.
Partake of wheat's breath.
Bread of your lips, shaped by gods.

Eat to the full: tortillas, *pan rustico.*
Leavened, kneaded: bread of dawn.
Pillars of yeast, rising, rising.

Wives

"I, unfortunately, was not a faithful husband.
I was always encountering women too desirable
to resist." [3]

Diego Rivera, *My Art, My Life: An Autobiography*
(with Gladys March)

I Angelina Beloff

In France, I fell in love
with the robust artist.

Though he rarely spoke of marriage,
one day he surprised me

with a wedding ring—
a gift from his mother.

I asked how he could cherish
a woman he refused to wed.

Annoyed, he turned his back
and resumed sketching.

In time, my belly grew.
After the child's birth,

if the baby whimpered, Diego
threatened to get rid

of him. In the studio,
self-absorbed, he cursed

anyone who interrupted him.
First bronchitis, then flu

sickened our Dieguito.
You would have thought

a father, out of decency, would
remain by his son's bed.

Instead, he reveled for days
with friends in bars,

lifting a beer to Cubism.
When our boy died,

who do you suppose
suffered most?

I do not want to sound offensive.
Diego is not vile.

He simply cares more for his art
than for any woman.

II Lupe Marín

As a husband he was attentive—
in fact, very manly.

But he ignored paying bills
and seldom bought food.

He preferred to dole out money
to the Communists

and splurged on hand-carved idols.
He never lavished our girls

with gifts. We parted because
he cheated on me

with a model. I was angered
by this lack of respect.

Because he was well-known,
rich women adored him.

And yet he rarely took a bath.
He washes daily now

because he's older, and to gain
a mistress he must cleanse.

Over the years I've forgiven
him for his dalliances.

The only woman who matters
to Diego is his muse.

III Frida Kahlo

In twilight's crimson, Diego
pillows against my breast,

wraps the legend of amaranth
around my shoulders. I become

his mother. He, my child,
a *sapo-rana*: a toad-frog

with sagging skin. "Fisita,"
he sings, his large-set eyes

droopy, "you are a sparrow
soaring, your eyebrows feathery,

close-knit." He is my universe,
the meandering stars. I, his spider

monkey, lunge from tree to tree.
But my Buddha is never all mine.

A mask, a headdress: my refuge.
I embrace dogs, an eagle,

parakeets, macaws. I endure
his cathedral of blood-red lies.

His little Demerol girl
in a dead sleep flirts with lions,

black angels with broken
wings. I, the breath of rose,

the fragrance of lust. He is
my destiny, the whistle of wind.

IV Emma Hurtado

The sky opened like a Spanish fan.
Party hats covered the horns

of bulls tugging fiesta wagons.
El Popo in the distance

spewed a shroud over the plain.
Throughout the ceremony,

clouds split into crinkled confetti.
We embraced, and it was over—

no witnesses, our wedding kept
secret for a month.

*

A lump hardened, burned, sickened
Diego, his forehead

creased from worrying
about a cancer so bold

he couldn't stare it down.
"Will you go with me

to a country," Diego asked,
"where blooms of cobalt

can cure?" A blur, the long days
in a Russian hospital.

Nights coalesced into fists
that pounded at the wound.

Women doctors showered him
with attention. I didn't mind.

For a man with a heart like his,
he needed his emotions fed

so he could paint twilight over seas
pure as dahlias, opening.

*

In April, they told us he was cured,
but his failing eyes closed

as if he saw the mysteries within,
as if he heard a lark's

doleful notes. Alone, he traveled
to Guanajuato, weeping

as the town's ghosts spilled
out of crumbling mines,

out of hills that lifted spirits into
indigo skies of his youth.

*

I dreamt his soul floated
over the boyhood town.

The sound of blood leaving
his veins filled the streets

as his small hands painted sunsets
too durable to fade.

I smoothed the sleek hair, wiped
furrows from his brow.

*

I was never envious of his success
or of the other women.

His inability to make love
these past few years

never mattered. His eminence
as an artist shields him.

Frida Kahlo, *The Two Fridas (Las dos Fridas)*, 1939
Oil on canvas, 5′ 8½″ x 5′ 8½″
Museo Nacional de Arte Moderno, Instituto Nacional de Bellas Artes, Mexico City, D.F., Mexico

Photo Credit: Schalkwijk / Art Resource, NY

II

FRIDA KAHLO

1907-1954

"I am not sick. I am broken. But I am happy to be alive as long as I can paint."[4]

Frida Kahlo: The Brush of Anguish
by Martha Zamora
(Trans. Marilyn Sode)

Frida and Wet Nurse

You do not nourish me, though you offer your breasts,
A wet nurse,

while my real mother gives birth to a sister.
I do my duty. I sacrifice

Your milk bitter as oleander, I call you Nana.
a suckling infant at home,

I'd rather press my lips to clouds drizzling
shedding tears

over a maze of leaves, engorged veins
buoyant as breath.

feeding insects, giddy with song. Newly born:
Wiggling, you turn from me,

a praying mantis, a monarch sucking fluid from stalks.
obsidian eyes, empty.

Estranged, I refuse to knead your chest,
Disheveled universe,

releasing drops into my half-opened mouth.
crack open this shield.

Indian woman, why won't you remove your mask?
Reorder this life

As moon candles the stars, cradle me
saturated with providence

so I can fold back time and dream my mother
among splashes of rain,

nurses me, her milk—consecrated by a kiss—
spilling from a holy font.

The Wedding Fiesta

I

In a native skirt, blouse and *rebozo*
borrowed from the maid, I married
Diego in a civil ceremony.
Thinking it insane to choose a man
old enough to be my father,
Mother refused to attend the wedding.
Nothing will destroy my mood,
I thought, until I arrived at the fiesta.
Ex-wife Lupe hoisted my skirt,
ridiculed my limb crippled by polio.
I knocked her off-balance.
Diego pulled us apart.
Dispirited, I drank like a mariachi
and sang above the band
while Lupe's tiger howl dissolved.

II

Nothing will destroy my mood,
I vowed, as I consumed oyster stew.
Stimulated by mollusks, I eyed
the multi-layered cake, a sugar-paste
couple on top, white-icing doves
lording over saffron rice, stuffed
chilies, spicy *mole* sprinkled
with sesame seeds. The alcohol
and roar of trumpets dulled
my senses. Above the balcony
amid lingerie hung out to dry,
an ornamental pennant flapped:
"Long Live Love!"

III

My marriage has always been
wound tight like my art: *a ribbon*
around a bomb, Breton said,
magic and heartache blended.
As the party ended, I appeased
Diego by feeding him watermelon,
thin slivers of papaya, the black
seeds: temptresses luring him
like wide-eyed brides-to-be.
I thought nothing could destroy
my spirit, but as days turned
to weeks, I woke frightened
at seeing life split open. Scorned,
I separated into *las dos Fridas.*
A heavy pall of smoke descended
as the clock ticked down.

The Two Fridas (I): On the Border Line between Mexico and the United States

I stand on a pedestal before the Ford factory,
Waving a Mexican flag,
clinging to the possibility of a better life,
I pause on the border line,
my bold cigarette, fingerless gloves,
head slightly turned,
coral necklace something to gossip about
my culture ignored
at fancy parties, thrown by industrialists.
in Gringolandia,
By day, bosses blare commands at workers.
the atmosphere smug.
I do not belong in Detroit with its smokestacks
Far from the temple of gods,
and skyscrapers, iron-gray, devoid of windows.
far from my collection of idols,
Diego perches for hours atop scaffolding,
I pine for volcanic stone,
adorning walls with the churn and grind of machinery.
for the budding cactus and jasmine
How can he claim the human spirit thrives here,
spinning roots through soil.
his message throttled by censorship?
After the miscarriage I disappeared
On the edge of his life, I replicate
in sun's fiery throat,
a brick building against a landscape cluttered
the quarter moon lost in a blur.
by chimney stacks, their robotic appendages
Hanging onto my past,
stretched-out, this country's flag

I ignore the stars and stripes.
rippling overhead in dense smog.
I cling to green, white, red.
I operate like a generator. Plugged in, I march
In a frilly, pink dress, I rouge my cheeks
on command to orders barked on cue.
and light up this dirty little stage.

The Two Fridas (II): Collage, Manhattan

I can't bear another minute of these
Pretentious snobs,
gringachos putting on airs over cocktails.
the big shots crave liquor.
I hunger for Mexico's exotic cuisine,
I thirst for lime water,
for quesadillas, spun from squash blossoms.
a dessert of mango sorbet.
In Manhattan an arctic chill descends,
In a collage, I paste
Wall Street's Federal Hall looming dead-center.
a church, a stained-glass window,
While Diego kowtows to American progress,
serpentine $ around a cross,
I pay homage to socialites for their perfect
fuel pumps, smokestacks,
plumbing: lid propped wide-open on a toilet.
a thunderhead grabbing the fumes,
Hats off to the sports hero, posing as a trophy,
a movie star, glamorous,
gold-lit on a column. Hats off to the telephone,
aloft a faded dwelling,
wires winding through buildings like nooses.
the windows grim.
For the millions earned weekly,
On the inaugural site, I paste
hats off to the moneybags. Lined up, the masses
George Washington, stoic,
protest the city's waste, its spent greed spilling
patriotic reds weaving
from a garbage can. Hats off to the system
throughout the city.
that gobbles up the poor like candy.

I don't care to be somebody.
Against skyscrapers I hang my ruffled costume,
I could care less about socialites.
dangling like an albatross. How like Lady Liberty
Shrouded in fog,
to wave absently. How like her to keep her distance
the harbor statue disappears,
from the lonely and forlorn.
her eyes shut to a passing ship.

The Two Fridas (III): Sitting on a Wicker Bed with Ceramic Doll

Nothing but drab walls, barren.
An idle toy bed
No paintings or pottery. No clay gods
shoved in a corner:
lining the terra cotta floor. No children
no figurines
feed my needs. And so I collect dolls,
fill the empty cradle
redo ragged bodies, top each one
with a celestial smile
with a miniature wig, silken hair
plucked from air.
from a cherub. Destitute, I sit upright
No baptismal gown,
on a wicker bed, hued by humidity.
no tiny shoes to coddle.
Stale cigarette smoke clings to my skin.
Tucked away, a fetus in a jar:
You ask how I'm doing, my only companion
an ungodly curse
in this room: ceramic, unclad,
holding me captive
its oval eyes begging me to lower my blouse
and not letting go.
so its lips can draw nectar from my nipples.
I invoke a saint
Cruel Diego turns a blind eye. I refuse
out of unenviable grief.
to hold the inanimate object. Can't the Maestro see
I wait for the lilt of day.
I need more than dogs, a deer, my countless dolls?

Young Dimas Rosas, Deceased at Age Three

I robe you for Paradise,
surround you with marigolds.

Sleeping child, saintly
in a mantle, brown feet

bared from birth to death:
O how you loved

delphiniums and baby's breath
in the courtyard of my home,

your mother calling you
to her side as she swept

the walkway. I crown you,
array you like a king

in plush gold, paint your eyes
slightly open as if still alive

with wonder. The gladiolus,
spiritual blossoms in your hands,

spread as apricot wings
to lift you: an *angelito*

into blue skies far from
the judgment hall of our elders.

Frida Dialogues with Her Heart

Is it Diego who slices me
I want to cut him,
from the body, or did you
hollow each chamber,
crop your raven hair short,
cast him aside like spoiled meat.
manlike, and then slash me
I want to rip out my heart,
from the chest? Iron-red streams
feel nothing, all those women
pour into the ocean
in his lustful embrace.
and flush to sea. I am
No longer clothed like a Mexican,
still beating: a nautilus
I abandon him,
cast ashore. My melodies
flee to New York City,
fade as you break down—
take lovers: men, women.
your school uniform and
I want to hurt him,
native garb dangling from ropes.
but what does he know of pain?
Wearing a plain skirt,
My foot bandaged, toes gone,
a tawny jacket flashy
at times I dress like a man,
with splotches of white, you
roam streets,
do nothing as clouds pull
my dreams without him:
demons into shivering sky.

center stage.

Let me back inside. Let me

Long into night

sever the cords

I drink brandy,

holding your beloved apparel,

curse my sister for giving in

throw out the liquor, lovers

to his advances.

doleful cries. Do not

Heart. Oh, Heart.

abandon me like an Aztecan child

Tear yourself free

sacrificed to the gods.

so I can live again.

The Two Fridas (IV)

As a child I met my imaginary friend

I have always known there are two of me:

in the earth's core. O how she made me laugh.

Dark-skinned Mexican. My German self,

Before each secret romp, I blew on a window

strong-willed, blouse ripped open, heart undone,

in my room, the pane misty like blurry soap bubbles.

scarlet flowers smeared on my skirt,

With my fingertip I drew a door, jumped through

its alabaster landscape stained. I clamp a vein.

to Pinzón. Entering the store's giant O, I crawled

My indigenous sister clasps my hand,

into world's interior where a playmate opened her arms,

her other hand encircling a portrait: frog prince,

listened to my secret problems, consoled me,

Diego as a boy. He lusts for the Mexican.

made me laugh despite my burdens.

His soul's yoked to hers. That's

When it was time to leave, I erased the magical door

what tears us apart: veins, tethered, choke me,

from the glassy surface. I wandered to the patio

our lives: aborted and miscarried.

to sit beneath a cedar tree's dancing shadows

Stop this flow of shared blood. Loosen this grip.

to conjure her up again, sturdy as breath.

The Two Fridas (V): The Wounded Table

"... behold the hand of him that betrayeth me
is with me on the table."
Luke 22:21

I was 33 when Diego requested a divorce.
Notice innocent

Time stopped at 2:53. Today I sit
children and a fawn nearby,

at the center of a wooden table, surrounded by
a terra cotta idol, peg legged—

remnants of a faltering life:
a papier-mâché Judas,

my sister Cristi's adoring children.
the sky heavy with clouds

My pet deer Granizo, his spots tiny
like puddles of hailstones.

like bread scraps. It is dinnertime, but I refuse to eat.
Notice how Judas's arm caresses me

Nor do I speak to the giant figure to my right,
as if flirting with death,

clothed in overalls, hands flattened on the surface.
droplets oozing from the laced ruffle

I am one with the Pre-Columbian idol to the left.
of my mestizo attire,

A skeleton entwines my unbound tresses around his wrist.
my wounded right foot hidden,

I refuse to give in to the harsh yank
the tabletop's piney knots wine-stained

or to care about blood pooling around the feet
as if bludgeoned,

of my companions. This is how my husband leaves me:
a stigma. Marked like a leper,

abused by a predatory disease. I reach out
I paint the frailty of my condition.

of my stupor, tug at the ponderous curtains until
I am surrounded by Diego's artifacts,

the tassels loosen and the burgundy sheaths fall,
a sacrificial fawn,

innocent as lambs, the passion play
no bread, no wine.

welling up inside me like a betrayal.
How could he undo me?

The Skeleton on Top of Frida's Four-Poster Bed

It seemed natural to affix the fearsome thing,

Ready to explode

laced with firecrackers, to the bed's canopy top.

on Sábado de Gloria,

Amused, Diego called the bony figure

Iscariot,

my immortal lover. Once, I calmed a friend

mortified—

who strayed into the bedroom for a peek,

a ritual—

the papier-mâché Judas sneering

hangs in effigy.

as if ready to bound from its perch.

Grimacing,

I suppose it sounds perverse, but I derive

burning

comfort from the skeleton, and so it stays put,

like a scapegoat,

caressing an armful of lavender and pink flowers.

the form shrivels,

At night it dreams, as I do, and soars like a spirit

thin shreds of paper

through blinding haze. My vine-covered bedspread

spiraling

trails a verdant hue as we start to tango. And why not

out of control.

dance with death, close as I've come to dying?

Frida and Black Cat

Enthroned in a wilderness of leaves
and butterflies, gelid as pins,

I see into the hearts of humans,
my luminous eyes possessed.

I hypnotize, draw you into my lair.
With a glassy gaze, I pull you closer.

In a primeval forest, I disappear
into a shadow's embrace.

A choker of thorns pierces my neck,
tenacious as a mortal wound.

Caught in a swarm of insects,
I lean into the flora.

I do not fear the witches' companion:
black cat, arched like a foe and protective

I seek solace by a woman's side.
I offer comfort to the childless one,

like the amulet, dangling from the neck,
a hummingbird cross-shaped.

detached as if undone, unmoved
by the whir of dragonflies.

Lustful as the monkey fondling my twig
necklace, noble feline with mirrored sight,

Startled by a noise, I hiss and curve
into an O, become a deity, proud.

look into my eyes, fixed as stone.
Stare back until you heal me.

On the Pedregal: Frida and Vines

On volcanic rock, I lie down,
stems unfurling from my breast

Curling out of ourselves, we envelop
your body. A river of green vines

onto desert terrain, cracked by
lava's flow. Here, I am whole.

stretched-out like a desert,
we wander the landscape,

I hunger for earth's fissures.
My arteries give birth to stones

agaves and cacti missing
from this arid place, the wind

exhaling legends and lore. I am one
with the chasms and rifts. I am one with

embracing thirsty leaves while tendrils
dig for moisture. Unrelenting:

the Holy Spirit, housed in my reclining
form. I feel the steely past dissolve

these ravines, their secrets
locked up like death's mysteries.

like a wound, stitched tight. When I
die, I will give life to bougainvillea,

Her need to feel close entraps us.
She sprawls out like creeping fig.

bleeding heart, and jasmine, cradled
beneath the rugged, harsh surface

She licks dew from our lips,
tastes the nectar on our skin.

until the plants spiral upward
and fan impurities from this plain.

She imagines our bodies
swimming in rain.

Portrait of Luther Burbank

Into a chamber of clouds,
Beside a brick pathway,

I sprout like a bountiful tree,
the roses curl toward dawn.

roots burrowed deep
Do not cut them.

in a steep gorge.
Sniff the fragrant petals.

I do not mind the aroma
The alluring scents

of decay beneath soil's crust.
swell into day. Like magic

Death tames, sweetens loam
the cross-breeder of corn,

with brittle bones.
trains ears to thicken,

Death loosens clay,
grafts giant cherries

fattens flowers, grains.
to mother trees.

Some call me Sorcerer, but I am
Golden russets

nothing more than nature's partner,
he gives to farmers.

sharing secrets: half-man,
He creates savory plumcots,

half-tree cultivating
tangy blackberries,

the mottled land.
enchanted quince in jams.

The distant hills, fertile, fatten
"Grow quickly, Walnut tree,"

with plums, peaches, nectarines.
he says, weaving a spell over

O Mighty Earth, with the wave of a hand
the garden. Overnight

I give to the multitudes my
robust leaves branch out:

fleshy vegetables and ripening fruits.
the hardwood towers into sky.

The Two Fridas (VI): Broken Column and Plaster Cast

Fragmentos, that's all that remains of my spine,
crumbling like an ancient column.

I swab a plaster cast with yellow,
violet, and mercurochrome.

Confined by a rigid brace, I look into a mirror,
iron nails boring their precision into flesh,

I dab red paint on the surface until
a hammer and sickle shine.

the pupils of my eyes strained, tears blurring
my sight. Two doves stare back.

Caged, I embellish each prison
made of leather, metal, or plaster.

How tired I am of surgeons tearing me
apart with their opinions and solutions,

To place me in a corset, doctors
suspend me from a cable.

splitting open the torso to reveal burdens I bear.
My husband's seldom at home, his art a ruse

I lose consciousness and imagine Diego
sketching a model draping herself,

luring him to paint long hours while I stand
here, nearly naked on the vast desert plain

swirling a sheet around the body
this simple, yet modest movement

he adores, white cloth draped over
my longing, earth's floor fractured

a siren's call to a life made of steel.
I listen to my world shattering.

as if by an earthquake. How demanding
to play the role of a brave child.

I call out to the void, wait
for the solace of an echo.

Why can't I collapse
like the fabled ruins of antiquity?

Frida and Mask

Who holds my face against her face?
Dumbstruck,

My stringy wig, violet,
hair piled high

conceals her stony gaze.
above a curtained glare

She'd rather be enclosed
veiled as in mourning,

in a garden of pitahayas and plums,
Diego's lost love,

lucent like plumage
a parrot with feathers

spread open. She steadies
unfurled, I fly into labyrinths

a tear-stained façade. Sable brows
of myself, scorn likenesses

and eyes herald a masquerade.
in self-portraits,

How like her to appear detached.
belittle the latest mistress,

Those slender fingers, tips polished red,
her unquenchable desires.

hold me lifeless against a cavernous stare.
Take off the weeping mask.

Beware. The gouged holes,
Undo this camouflage.

pecked out as if by a ravenous crow,
Let them see the Concealer.

will numb you with a piercing cry.
Let them see who I really am.

Deer Running

Beneath a coarse sky, I flee
through an enclosed glade,

Run toward the light,
little deer. Catch hold of

my limber frame: a young stag's
crowned with massive antlers.

brightness sizzling above
the glazed, forest floor.

Arrows gash my chest and flank.
Crimson trickles from wounds,

Raw sienna spools
a well-worn path

my pursuer crouched behind a tree,
the trunk's exposed roots swollen

in the distance. Birdsong
pulses like waves bobbing

like the flawed design of my human
form, stones in my soul.

crystal notes. Run toward
the hymns, nimble deer.

And you, Diego, place one leafy,
golden branch withering before me

Let loose your foe's nine arrows,
trembling in your hide.

as I prepare to die and resurrect
as growth: green bark,

Do not fear death. Your wounds,
their indelible marks will heal

green branches at the foot
of your shadow,

as I push away lightning
from the barren plot,

swallowed whole
by sun's unerring rays.

where your body collapses
in a radiant spool.

The Two Fridas (VII): Paint Me Flying

"It is certain they are going to amputate my right leg. . . .
I am very, very worried, but at the same time
I feel it would be a relief."[5]

THE DIARY OF FRIDA KAHLO, August 1953

Paint me flying through saffron skies:
Feet—why do I want them?

a hummingbird, wavering like a supple leaf.
Wings are enough.

Balanced on a sliver of dawn,
I'll wear a wooden leg

I'll hover among trumpet vines.
and twirl on a dare—

Paint me curled up in a seamless knot:
among honeysuckle, bee balm—

a hairless caterpillar on a pansy's back,
slender as a flicker.

waving its gilded wand until a butterfly flits.
I'll don leather boots,

Paint me reclining on a mandrake's tongue,
cerise aflame,

stout as a root. Paint me ascending, a parrot
graced with bells.

from a basket of berries, luscious in a heap.
If I have wings,

Píntame volando, a dragonfly plaiting the air.
what do I need feet for?

Letter to Diego

What is it that connects us? You said
you loved me in my Tehuana dress.
You said you loved my black hair
secured with steel-red ribbons and combs
and buckling like a braided snake.
How long did it take you to become
a maelstrom around my neck, swirling
waters spun into a silken noose
and tightening? I cannot deny my anger.
Your world teems with other women:
your model Nahui, then Cristina, my own
sister. How could you? The thought
of you sleeping with others changes
my heart into an hourglass that empties
into the veins of every woman
you've bedded. I cannot deny my hurt.
You gave me child after child, each torn
from my womb, umbilical cords spiraling
out of me like groundless roots.
After my third baby died, the doctor
cut off my toes while you, selfish
and callous, painted pretty Cristina
into your *Epic of the Mexican People,*
her two children seated beside her
covering me with their oblivion.
And so I loosened my long hair,
sheared it to take you down with me
where I lay exposed, blood-splattered.
How much can a person endure?
I lie, immobile, in my four-poster bed,
the past unraveling like one of your murals.
Some people suffer a single tragedy,
but I have suffered two. After the first—

a bus accident—I remember hearing
voices, a handrail piercing my body,
the severed organs spilling
a communion of blood. You, Diego,
are my other tragedy. I would tear you,
piece by piece, from my heart,
but I have nearly lost my soul.
I can no longer bear loneliness,
your affairs, your lies. And yet—
my leg shorn from me like a lost ribbon,
my spine a withered branch—when I die,
I will fly back to you on gilt wings.

The Crematorium at the Panteón Civil de Dolores

I

Never question my power
or assume I delight in what I do.
I can excite, ignite, or illuminate
bodies. For hours, they burn
with a fervor that reduces
to an impenetrable gray mass.
Do not label the remains "ashes."
Gather a fistful of these bone
fragments, ground into a fine
substance sacred as dust.
Place a loved one in a treasured
cloth to preserve in a cedar box
where memory cannot die
until mind or time releases
it from your grasp.

II

Resting on a cart, Frida Kahlo
approached the oven with royal
dignity, her headband lined
with carnations scarlet as roses,
a shawl gracing the sloped shoulders.
When they rolled her through
my doors, a blaze roared,
thrust her upright, hair haloed,
the vermilion scars all over
her back aglow. Like a phoenix
she burned. The ardor of her
trembling built to a crescendo
as the inferno intensified,
her face a sunflower in bloom.
Once the flames subsided,
her skeleton emerged,
intact, lustrous as silver.

III

Unlike the arsonist who derives
pleasure from torching, I value
the artistry of fire and consume
those disfigured by disease
or injuries too severe to mask.
I ignite the forlorn and those
who cannot bear lying
prone for eternity.

IV

Who can fault Diego for
sketching the filigreed bones?
No longer confined to a bed,
Frida burned with zeal—
no need for vibrant jewels,
skirts trimmed with flounces,
no want of *huipiles* or hair
plaited with ribbons and flowers.
In the comfort of an oven,
she became whole again.

La Casa Azul

Blue, the aura of my walls: a deep-matte
añil so intense it wards off evil.

Nothing can compare to this uncloaked
hue, neither Michoacán earthenware,

nor sapphire streamers billowing
from beaks of papier-mâché jays.

Neither floating teal boats nor hand-blown
royal goblets can compare

to the spell I cast: *añil* regal in *retablos*
and gossamer in glazed Talavera tiles.

Alluring: *añil* peeling off the courtyard
terrace amid songbirds' warbles,

the chatter of parrots, the steely barks
of hairless dogs, their skin slate-blue.

Always at dusk, Frida arrived home, beguiling,
costumed in violet-blue.

The hall mirror reflected my longtime
occupant, her indigo jewels, jangling,

her throaty laughter, euphoric, pouring
out of windows into narrow streets

of Coyoacán, rushing into azure lakes,
rivers, crossing borders—

a blue tapestry like a talisman falling from sky,
even more seductive than before.

Notes & Glossary

I DIEGO RIVERA—1886-1957

[1]The epigraph that introduces the first section of the book is from Diego Rivera's *My Art, My Life: An Autobiography* (with Gladys March). New York: Dover Publications, Inc., 1991, p. 41. (ISBN: 0-486-26938-8)

"Diego and Calla Lilies": after *Calla Lily Vendor (Vendedora de alcatraces),* 1943 and *Nude with Calla Lilies (Desnudo con alcatraces)*, 1944. Rivera painted the calla lily so often in connection with women that the flower became an erotic or sensual symbol in his art.

peso: unit of currency

petate: reed

"Stone Worker and Creviced Rock": after *Stone Worker (Picapedrero)*, 1943

"The Milliner and His Hats": after *The Milliner (El modista)*—Portrait of Henri de Chatillon, 1944

"Halley's Comet":

Porfirio Díaz: dictator of Mexico (1877-1880 and 1884-1911)

Carmen Romero Rubio de Díaz: wife of Porfirio Díaz

muy importante: very important

la crema de la sociedad: the cream of the society

Angelina Beloff: Rivera's common-law wife with whom he lived in Europe from 1911-1921. Beloff gave birth to a son, Diego in 1916. Two years later the son died.

Marevna Vorobiev-Stebelska: Rivero left Beloff for six months in 1917 to live with Marevna, who gave birth to his daughter, Marika, in 1919.

campesinos: peasants; countrymen; farmers; Indians

"Zapatista Landscape: The Guerilla": after *Zapatista Landscape—The Guerilla (Paisaje zapatista—El guerrillero)*, 1915

Emiliano Zapata: Considered a national hero, this leading figure in the 1910 Mexican Revolution fought to dismantle the dictatorship of Porfirio Díaz. Rivera's cubist painting pays homage to the peasant revolt and reveals the artist's growing political sensibility.

mestizo: mixed-race

MURALS
(Location: Secretaría de Educación Pública in Mexico City, Mexico)

I **"Entering the Mine"**: after *Entering the Mine (Entrada a la mina)*, Court of Labor, 1923

mi padre: my father

II **"Leaving the Mine"**: after *Leaving the Mine (Salida de la mina)*, Court of Labor, 1923

III **"Hymn: The Embrace"**: after *The Embrace (El abrazo)*, Court of Labor, 1923

mis hermanos: my brothers

IV **"The Festival Workers Address Corn"**: after *The Maize Festival (La fiesta del maíz)*, Court of the Fiestas, 1923-24

V **"Offerings, Day of the Dead"**: after *The Sacrificial Offering, Day of the Dead (La ofrenda, Día de muertos)*, Court of the Fiestas, 1923-24

Posada: José Guadalupe Posada was an influential Mexican artist known for his *calaveras*, or sugar skulls, associated with the festival, Day of the Dead. His most famous creation is Calavera Catrina.

pescado y pollo picante: fish and spicy chicken

danza de la muerte: dance of death

VI **"City Festival, Day of the Dead"**: after *Day of the Dead (Día de muertos)*, Court of the Fiestas, 1923-1924

pulque: a fermented drink made from maguey sap

los muertos: the dead

VII **"The Burning of the Judases"**: after *The Burning of the Judases (La quema de los Judas)*, Court of the Fiestas, 1923-24

VIII **"Night of the Rich"**: after *The Orgy (La orgía)*, Court of the Fiestas, 1926

casa grande: large house

inocente: innocent; naïve

pesos duros: hard-earned money

IX **"Night of the Poor"**: after *Night of the Poor* or *The Dream (La noche de los pobres o el sueño)*, Court of the Fiestas, 1926

pan fresco, por favor: fresh bread, please

María, Madre de Dios: Mary, Mother of God

X **"Bread"**: after *Our Bread (El pan nuestro)*, Court of the Fiestas, 1928
[2]The epigraph is from *Guia de los Murales de Diego Rivera en la Secretaría de Educación Pública.* Text by Antonio Rodriguez. 1986, p. 95.

pan rustico: rustic-style Spanish bread

WIVES
[3]The epigraph that introduces "Wives" is from Diego Rivera's *My Art, My Life: An Autobiography* (with Gladys March). New York: Dover Publications, Inc., 1991, p. 83. (ISBN: 0-486-26938-8)

I & II **"Angelina Beloff"** and **"Lupe Marín"**: Both poems are monologues loosely inspired by comments attributed to Rivera's common-law wife and his second wife. [From: Rivera, Diego. *My Art, My Life: An Autobiography* (with Gladys March), Appendix, pp. 183-186.]

Lupe Marín: also known as Guadalupe Marín

III **"Frida Kahlo"**:

sapo-rana: toad-frog, one of Kahlo's affectionate nicknames for Rivera

IV **"Emma Hurtado"**:

El Popo: the abbreviated form of *Popocatépetl*, an active volcano, southeast of Mexico City.

Guanajuato: the town of Diego's birth, known for its silver mines.

II FRIDA KAHLO: 1907-1954

[4]The epigraph for the second section of the book is from a statement Frida Kahlo made to reporters of *Time* magazine on the occasion of her first solo exhibition in Mexico in 1953 (*Galería de Arte Contemporáneo*). [From: Zamora, Martha. *Frida Kahlo: The Brush of Anguish.* Trans. Marilyn Sode. San Francisco: Chronicle Books LLC, ©1990, p. 126. Used with permission of Chronicle Books LLC, San Francisco. Visit ChronicleBooks.com]

"Frida and Wet Nurse": after *My Nurse and I (Mi nana y yo)*, 1937

"The Wedding Fiesta": Kahlo and Rivera married on August 21, 1929.

Pieter Brueghel (also Bruegel): a 16th century Flemish painter

rebozo: wrap; shawl

mole: black chili sauce

las dos Fridas: the two Fridas

"The Two Fridas (I): On the Border Line between Mexico and the United States": after *Self-Portrait on the Border Line between Mexico and the United States (Autorretrato en la frontera entre México y Estados Unidos)*, 1932

gringolandia: the United States

"The Two Fridas (II): Collage, Manhattan": after *My Dress Hangs There (Mi vestido cuelga ahí)*, 1933

"The Two Fridas (III): Sitting on a Wicker Bed with Ceramic Doll": after *Self-Portrait on the Bed* or *Me and My Doll (Yo y mi muñeca)*, 1937

"Young Dimas Rosas, Deceased at Age Three": after *The Young Dimas Rosas Deceased at Age Three (El difuntito Dimas)*, 1937

marigold: the flower of death

angelito: little angel

"Frida Dialogues with Her Heart": after *Memory, or the Heart (Recuerdo)*, 1937

"The Two Fridas (IV)": after *The Two Fridas (Las dos Fridas)*, 1939

"The Two Fridas (V): The Wounded Table": after *The Wounded Table (La mesa herida)*, 1940

"The Skeleton on Top of Frida's Four-Poster Bed": after *The Dream (El sueño)*, 1940

"Frida and Black Cat": after *Self-Portrait with Thorn Necklace and Hummingbird (Autorretrato)*, 1940

"On the Pedregal: Frida and Vines": after *Roots* or *The Pedregal (Raíces)*, 1943

"Portrait of Luther Burbank": after *Luther Burbank*, 1931

"The Two Fridas (VI): Broken Column and Plaster Cast": after *Broken Column (La columna rota)*, 1944 and *Plaster Cast with Hammer and Sickle (La escayola con la hoz y el martillo)*, 1950

fragmentos: fragments

"Frida and Mask": after *The Mask (La máscara)*, 1945

"Deer Running": after *The Little Deer (La venadita)*, 1946

"The Two Fridas (VII): Paint Me Flying": after *Feet What Do I Need Them for if I Have Wings to Fly (Pies, para qué los quiero si tengo alas pa'*

volar), 1953, an illustration in Kahlo's diary. [Note: Only one leg was amputated below the knee.]
[5]The epigraph comes from *THE DIARY OF FRIDA KAHLO.* English translation copyright ©2005. New York: Harry N. Abrams, Inc., p. 277. Used by permission of Harry N. Abrams, Inc., New York. All rights reserved.

mandrake root: considered a cure for infertility

Píntame volando: Paint me flying

"Letter to Diego": This poem was inspired by Kahlo's *Accident (Accidente)*, 1926; *Self-Portrait with Her Hair Cut Off (Autorretrato de pelona)*, 1940; *Self-Portrait with Plait (Autorretrato con trenza)*, 1941; and by Rivera's *Epic of the Mexican People (Epopeya del pueblo mexicano)* in the fresco cycle, 1929-35.

Tehuana dress: Kahlo wore the native garb of the Isthmus of Tehuantepec to please Diego, who valued her indigenous heritage. The ruffled skirt hid her leg shriveled by polio. The embroidered blouse completed the elegant costume.

Nahui Olín: one of Diego's models

"The Crematorium at the Panteón Civil de Dolores":

huipiles: embroidered blouses

"La Casa Azul":

añil: indigo

retablos: altarpieces

Coyoacán: a suburb of Mexico City, where Kahlo lived for most of her life in the Blue House, or *La Casa Azul*

Sources Consulted

During the research phase I gleaned helpful information about the lives and artwork of Rivera and Kahlo from a variety of books (print editions):

Alcántara, Isabel, and Sandra Egnolff. *Frida Kahlo and Diego Rivera.* Munich: Prestel, 1999.

Bauer, Claudia. *Frida Kahlo.* Munich: Prestel, 2007.

THE DIARY OF FRIDA KAHLO: An Intimate Self-Portrait. Intro. Carlos Fuentes. Commentary. Sarah M. Lowe. New York: Harry N. Abrams, Inc., ©2005.

Diego Rivera: A Retrospective. Ed. Cynthia Newman Helms. New York: W. W. Norton & Company, ©1986.

Drucker, Malka. *Frida Kahlo.* Albuquerque: University of New Mexico Press, ©1991.

Frida by Frida. Foreword. Raquel Tibol. Tran. Gregory Dechant. México: Editorial RM, 2006.

Frida Kahlo Retrospective. Exhibition concept by Helga Prignitz-Poda. Munich: Prestel, ©2010.

Grimberg, Salomon. *Frida Kahlo: Song of Herself.* London and New York: Merrell Publishers, 2008.

Grimberg, Salomon. *Frida Kahlo: The Still Lifes.* London and New York: Merrell Publishers, 2008.

Guia de los murales de Diego Rivera en la Secretaría de Educación Pública. Presentation and Text. Antonio Rodriguez. México: SEP, 1984.

Hamill, Pete. *Diego Rivera.* New York: Harry N. Abrams, Inc., ©1999.

Herrera, Hayden. *Frida: A Biography of Frida Kahlo.* New York: Perennial, ©1983.

Herrera, Hayden. *Frida Kahlo: The Paintings.* New York: Perennial, ©1991.

Herrera, Hayden. *Frida: Una biografía de Frida Kahlo.* México: Editorial Diana, 1984.

Homenaje a Diego Rivera Retratos. Mexico City: Dolores Olmedo Patiño Foundation, 2007.

Kettenmann, Andrea. *Diego Rivera.* Köln: Taschen, ©2006.

Kettenmann, Andrea. *Frida Kahlo: Pain and Passion.* Köhn: Taschen, ©2003.

The Letters of Frida Kahlo: Cartas Apasionadas. Compiled by Martha Zamora. San Francisco: Chronicle Books LLC, ©1995.

Marín, Guadalupe Rivera. *Diego Rivera the Red.* Houston, TX: Arte Público Press, ©2004.

Marnham, Patrick. *Dreaming with His Eyes Open: A Life of Diego Rivera.* Berkeley and Los Angeles: University of California Press, ©1998.

Milner, Frank. *Frida Kahlo.* London: PRC Publishing Ltd, ©1990.

Rivera, Diego (with Gladys March). *My Art, My Life: An Autobiography.* New York: Dover Publications, Inc., 1991.

Rivera, Guadalupe, and Marie-Pierre Colle. *Frida's Fiestas.* New York: Clarkson Potter/ Publishers, ©1994.

Tibol, Raquel. *Frida Kahlo: An Open Life.* Trans. Elinor Randall. Albuquerque: University of New Mexico Press, ©1993.

Wolfe, Bertram D. *The Fabulous Life of Diego Rivera.* New York: Cooper Square Press, 2000.

Zamora, Martha. *Frida Kahlo: The Brush of Anguish.* Trans. Marilyn Sode. San Francisco: Chronicle Books LLC, ©1990.

About the Author

Carolyn Kreiter-Foronda served as Poet Laureate of the Commonwealth of Virginia from 2006-2008. She holds a B.A. from Mary Washington College, now the University of Mary Washington, and a M.Ed., M.A. and a Ph.D. from George Mason University, where she received the institution's first doctorate. In 2007 both universities gave her the Alumna of the Year Award.

She has published five books of poetry and co-edited two poetry anthologies. Her poems have been nominated for six Pushcart Prizes and appear throughout the United States and abroad in magazines, such as *Nimrod, Prairie Schooner, Mid-American Review, Hispanic Culture Review, El Quetzal, Best of Literary Journals, Poet Lore,* and *An Endless Skyway,* an anthology of poems by U.S. State Poets Laureate.

Her numerous awards include five grants from the Virginia Commission for the Arts; a *Spree* First Place award; multiple awards in Pen Women competitions; a Special Merit Poem in *Comstock Review's* Muriel Craft Bailey Memorial contest; a *Passages North* contest award; an Edgar Allan Poe first-place award; a Virginia Cultural Laureate Award; and a Resolution of Appreciation from the State Board of Education for her contributions as Poet Laureate of Virginia.

She currently serves as a Literary Arts Specialist on a Metrorail Public Art Project, which will integrate poems, including her own, into art installations at metro stations in Northern Virginia. Carolyn is an accomplished visual artist, whose works have been widely displayed. As an adjunct faculty member, she teaches art-inspired poetry workshops for the Virginia Museum of Fine Arts.

OTHER BOOKS BY CAROLYN KREITER-FORONDA

Contrary Visions
Gathering Light
Death Comes Riding
Greatest Hits, 1981—2000
River Country

ANTHOLOGIES

In a Certain Place
Co-edited with Alice Marie Tarnowski

Four Virginia Poets Laureate: A Teaching Guide
Co-edited with Edward W. Lull